Before
The Wedding

365 Things to Think About
Before You Marry

ISBN 978-0-692-53233-1

Printed in the United States of America

Published by:

Universal City Creations
529 Elkins Ave.
Elkins Park, PA 19027
www.suziewrites.com

The most important decision you make is WHO YOU CHOOSE TO MARRY. Love at first sight happens. Long friendships become long marriages. Some marriages end quickly, others last until the kids leave home, and the best last forever.

You would get lots of information about a job before you'd take it. You'd get many recommendations before you hire someone to do a job for you. So why wouldn't you put serious thought and energy into choosing a person to share your life and children?

Look before you leap! Think before you leap!

Love your intended enough to discuss all the pages of this daily journal together.

Strong relationships raise healthy children and contribute to positive, constructive communities. You deserve the best. Review your journal every anniversary.

Watch how your love grows.

ACKNOWLEDGMENTS

~ My gratitude to all my clients that I talked
to, and learned from in twenty-two years as a
sales rep.

~ Love forever to Nancy Gold who blessed me
with the means to make
BEFORE THE WEDDING happen.

~ Jewels in the crown of the soul of
Robin Morgan for her beautiful artistic gifts,
wisdom and love.

~ Blessings ten-fold to Amy Collins
at New Shelves for believing in
BEFORE THE WEDDING and launching it.

~ To everyone who reaches for the perfected
expression of love.

Journal of

Date

Before The Wedding

By

Suzanne Salas

Cover design by Robin G. Morgan

Edited by Anne Stremanos

Published by

Universe City Creations

www.suziewrites.com

Other books by Suzanne Salas, *Bless My Soul*

To Baxter, Albert and Paul.

Until we meet again...

How does your love treat their* parents? Do
they speak kindly to them? About them? Are
they thoughtful? How will they treat YOUR
mother and father?

Do you LIKE their family? This is important.
They created the person you love.

Is your partner from a different culture?   If
so, run to the Internet and get information
on their customs and beliefs. It may seem
exotic at first, but reality is that cultures may
clash. Will you be considered property? Will
you share equally? How will your children be
raised? You need to have a clear
understanding on these issues.

*For English grammar sticklers the gender neutral singular "they" and "their" has been chosen over the awkward "he/she".

Do you enjoy sharing meals? Are they an opportunity to communicate? After a while bad table manners, or silence will wear on you. Be brave. Talk about this now and work on it.

Are you a neat nick? Is your partner a slob? Or vice versa? It can work, but you need to agree on what you both can tolerate.

Is there any chance of hereditary illness that could affect your children? If so seek genetic counseling. Call your local hospital for information. You will be glad you did. The more you know the better off you all will be.

What do you expect of marriage? Talk about it. Make a list. Do your expectations mesh? If not, you need to work out your differences to avoid future clashes.

What are your career goals? Discuss this. How will you both achieve them? Taking turns? Loans? Will you complete your educations before you marry?

Is it important to you to have a strong spiritually compatible relationship? There is a website called MatchingSpirit.com. Review the questions they ask. The more you have in common the better.

What is your spiritual outlook? Your faith?
This is very important. Life is full of
challenges. What helps you cope and go on?
If you are very young, it's time to look around
and find a spiritual support group you both
like. It's true that the family that prays
together, stays together.

Is your partner enthusiastic about life? Do
your energies match? The older you become,
the less flexible you are to change. How will
you blend?

Do you want to have children? How many?
Why? What are your child raising ideas? Education? Discipline? Will you share
child-rearing tasks?

Is your partner moody and sometimes depressed? Can you live with this? Seek medical advice and learn all you can. Some people have glitches in their bodies that need attention. Don't waste time. Get help.

Pre-marital counseling is a good thing. You check a road map before you go on a trip. Be flexible. Talking about how to join two lives is a good thing.

Love is NEVER violent! Love means wanting the best for the people in your life.

Would you want to be abused either physically or emotionally? If this happens, run for an exit and move forward with your life. Loving yourself means NOT allowing others to hurt you.

Marriage vows say "...in sickness and in health." It is easy to love a healthy person. Can you be there for your partner as you want them to be there for you? The unexpected can hit hard and fast. Love is a powerful healing energy.

Does your partner talk to you about everything? Lack of communication will destroy your relationship. Be open. Be brave. Silence is for the grave. Hint for men: women want conversation.

Do you punish with silence or by walking out or screaming? Look at these things. Observe how your partner's family handle disagreements.

Picture your partner aging. An old couple still sitting hand in hand is a beautiful thing. Work at your marriage, and that will be you someday.

Does fat, bald, short, or wrinkled bother you? Let's hope it doesn't bother the person who loves you.

How different is your partner's faith? Will this separate you in time? Will it cause problems with your families? Discuss how you will live with different faiths or blend them.

How will you raise your children in different faiths? This should be settled before you marry. Children need guidance and a spiritual foundation.

❦

Some men choose to not wear a wedding ring. Millions of marriages have endured without men wearing a ring, because their commitment is solid. You need to discuss this issue if you anticipate a problem.

❦

Do you listen to what he or she is really saying? Start right away to say what you mean. Don't play mind games. Life is difficult enough. Communicate clearly.

How good are you at compromising? How about your partner? Can you both put your wants and desires aside now and then? Are you both fair? Sometimes one gives more than the other. Talk about this now.

✧

It is VITAL that you both have friends. Friendship is practice for marriage. Meet and talk to your partner's friends. Are they people you want to be around?

✧

Do your friends like your partner? If they don't they are trying to tell you something. LISTEN. Friends help support a marriage.

What side of the double, queen or king size bed do you want to sleep on? Research shows that men hear better out of their right ear. So gals, choose the right side.

Is your partner a problem solver? Being the sole decision maker gets old fast.

What does friendship mean to you? Are you blessed to have found someone who is your defender, supporter and cheerleader? Are YOU a good friend?

A year from now you will not be the same
person you are now. Everyone changes
and grows. Plan to grow along with your
spouse. It is important to know that change
and growth will happen. Be prepared for it.

How about a date once a week after you are
married? Keep courting one another and keep
talking.

With the first child, a wife turns into a
mother who is responsible for keeping a
helpless being alive. Men need to know that
they may not feel as important for a time
after a baby comes. The best thing a new dad
can do is to get involved and be a supportive
husband and father. Your rewards will be
awesome!

Do you enjoy the same music? If not, get headsets. Technology is a wonderful thing.

⁂

If your partner is a sports nut and you are not, plan ahead. Can you be a sports widow or widower? There are lots of things to do in life. Talk about this now and make a plan.

⁂

How will you celebrate the holidays? Are they spiritually based for you, or a vacation? Whose family will you go to? Marriage is sharing, not going in different directions.

Does your fiancé share well?   When one
partner gives and the other only takes, there
is an imbalance.

⊰⊱

The words ALWAYS, FOREVER and NEVER
must be used with caution. They are
extremes.

⊰⊱

Do you like sex? There are thousands of books
about sex. Sex is the icing on the cake of marriage. It is sharing, giving, loving, and healing. Have questions? Read and learn together.

If you can't say "I love you" easily, start practicing. It is like the key to the door. How wonderful it feels to be told you are loved.

Can you tell a joke? Laugh at a joke? Laughter is the oil of the machine of life. Its ripples of energy keep us going.

Do you enjoy giving gifts? Tokens of appreciation are another way of saying I love you, and I appreciate you.

Remember the parents of your partner. Their love made and nurtured this person you love. Thanking them now and then on your spouse's birthday would be a thoughtful thing to do.

When children come into your life where will you go for Easter, Thanksgiving, Hanukah and Christmas? Every situation and family is different. Don't assume anything. Remember what is best for your family. Make sure everyone knows your plan.

Marriage is a responsibility. Therefore, having a will and life insurance is smart. Loving one another means caring for them.

How does your partner treat animals? A
person who mistreats an animal, may
mistreat you. Beware. Power over another
can be very destructive.

Is your intended an only child? Are
you? Unique attitudes, ideas, and
responsibilities come with only children. An
only child has both aging parents to consider.
An only child may expect special attention.
This will be interesting to discuss.

Who do you admire most and why? What
choices in life did this person make in life to
be admirable? Share this with your
partner. Enjoy learning what your
intended thinks about people.

Non-physical abuse methods are humiliation,
subtle slurs, statements with the intent to
make you feel worthless. This is not the way
anyone should treat another who they love.
You deserve to be treated with respect and
dignity, no abuse, contempt and put downs.

What type of home do you both want? This is
why it's important to begin thinking and
planning now.

Don't attempt to teach happiness or
success home. Love leaps around the
world. Children's minds are taught to
change. Try to be flexible, be accepting.

Non-physical abuse methods are humiliation, threats and put downs, with the intent to make you feel worthless. This is not the way anyone should live, and you don't need to. You deserve to be treated with respect. You are worthy of love. Get out and get help.

What type of home do you both want? How will you reach your goal? Begin dreaming and planning now.

Do you come from a "no touch" home or a "snuggle" home? Love leaps around this for a while. Childhood patterns are difficult to change. Try to be flexible. Reach out.

How do you feel about lending money to friends or family? Be united in this.

Do you need a prenuptial agreement? This is a contract arranged for the division of property, finances and support in the event of a divorce. Laws vary from state to state. This can be prepared by an attorney, or there are do-it-yourself forms on the Internet. There are also postnuptial agreements that can be made after you are married.

How well do you know your partner? Can you make social plans with friends without asking? Is this important to you?

Do you have a healthy balance of work and play? Schedule play as seriously as you do work.

How will you handle money? This is a huge issue. Will you have a budget? Will you each have your own accounts or separate accounts? Will you have credit accounts?

Discuss how you will decide on large item purchases. A home, cars, computers, new technology, sports equipment, furniture?

Do you have fun together? Do you make one another laugh? Humor keeps us alive and going.

Can you count on your partner to be there during rough times? There will be rough times and you will need one another.

Who can cook? Who wants to plan meals and cook? Ideally, both of you. This takes a large percentage of your time. Many hands make light work.

Eat out now and then to celebrate big and
little things.

Is your partner thoughtful? It's the little
things in life that count.
Say "Let me help you."

Take care of yourself. Have a yearly
physical check-up. Take advantage of tests
that prevent disease. Encourage one another
to see the dentist regularly. Walking and
talking together is healthy too.

Who is the boss? Is there one? Can you walk
in your marriage equally, side by side?
Besides, bossy people aren't very endearing.

Will the husband in your marriage be a house
husband? Do what works for you and your
family. Arrange your schedule according to
your needs and comfort.

Do you have a burning desire to travel to
many places? Not everyone wants to. Some
are content to live and vacation in the same
places every year. It's a good idea to talk about
this or maybe plan separate vacations.

Homebodies are just this. Find out where
your partner is most comfortable. If they
travel for work can you be content at home?
Absence doesn't always make the heart grow
fonder.

Is your partner a night owl, or morning
person? This difference may affect your
marriage. Learn one another's
energy patterns.

Children deserve their childhood. Their lives
come before their parents. Are you grown up
enough to be a parent?

Can your partner read a map or follow directions? Do you care? Save time. If your GPS fails, stop and ask for directions. It's not a crime!

What married couples do you admire and why? Can you ask them how they handle certain things in their marriage? We learn from example. Pay attention and take notes.

Love and security can be ONE idea to some. Think about this. Are you marrying for one, or the other, or both?

Is there a big difference in age between you
and your future spouse? How will your being
together enhance your lives?

Some people need to be entertained and
others are observers. Is one of you more
active?   Will you be able to enjoy your
differences?

Are you the second, third, fourth spouse?
Maybe it's smart to find out WHY the
marriages didn't work? This is not easy to ad-
dress. Often people keep repeating
behavior and patterns that doom a
marriage. Talk to family and friends. Gather
all the information you can. Don't let love
blind you. Pre-marriage counseling could be a
good thing.

Are you both optimists? Pessimists? Or one of each? What works for you? "Birds of a feather flock together." It can get old cheering up a partner all the time. On the other hand, a "down" person could get weary of a perpetual sunny person. What works for you?

⁂

Do you like your partner's parents' relationship? Talk about it. Do you want yours to be like it or not like it?

⁂

Was your education completed after high school? After college or advanced studies? Some people are life-long learners. Do you think about education the same way? This will be very important when you have children.

Do you have a fantasy about what your marriage will be like? Share it with your partner. Visualization can become a reality. This is a good thing to discuss so you both are in the same fantasy.

※

It should be, I love you therefore I need you, not I need you therefore I love you. Of course there is a bit of both in a relationship. Being loved and needed is so important.

※

An unhappy person is critical and judgmental of others. Do you want to be, or be with, someone who needs to build themselves up at the expense of others? "If you can't say something nice, don't say anything at all."

Is there alcoholism in the family? Read up on the hereditary markers that could affect your future and your children's. The cost and use of alcohol will overshadow every aspect of your life and will create mental, social, financial, health, and emotional damage and grief. Respect yourself and seek help to offer the best of you to another. Children of alcoholics have their own unique set of problems even if they do not drink.

Alcoholics, says Dr. Don Rosen, do not take lovers, they take hostages. Know what you are getting into if your partner drinks too much. Educate yourself. Talk to people who know about the effects of alcohol and drugs. There are big hurdles for the addicted and it could be worse for you. Love does not conquer all. No amount of love can make them stop. It is singularly their choice.

Agree to keep your intimate life between the two of you. It is unique and special. Glow in your love. Sharing personal experiences lessens them.

Do you trust him or her and your life.

Want type of wedding ... as your style itself. A
... together. Be realistic about your parents and
... for the issue in every moment of the day to
... self good ...
Don't drink too much. Dance with ... mind ...
... you ... can recall it often in the
...

... children for ... information from the
... dress wedding in response. Have it in
... book.

Do you trust him or her with your life?

What type of wedding fits your style best? A church wedding? Large or small guest list? Eloping? Be realistic about your parents and your finances. When the day comes focus, focus, focus on every moment of the day. It will go by very fast and will be a whirlwind. Don't drink too much. Dance with joy, and sear the day in your memory. Remember how you feel so you can recall it often in the years ahead.

Get a written recommendation from the mother of your soon-to-be spouse. Save it in this book.

Do you care if he goes out with the guys, and she with girlfriends now and then?

You can't have too many friends.

❧

Does he or she take advice best from men or women? That is, some women only value men's advice, or men value only women's advice. Parents had a big role in this. This is interesting to know.

❧

Does your partner hold a grudge? This gets old and is a waste of time. Talk about this. Holding a grudge is like taking a slow poison. It kills communication.

Is your partner fair? Can they weigh both
sides of a situation and be generous of spirit?

❧

How will you educate your children? Public,
private, home schooling? Your children's
future depends on your example and your
guidance. Remember that each child is
different.

❧

Make a list of places you'd both like to visit in
the world. Map it out. Dream and plan, then
enjoy the anticipation as well as the trip...
then the memories.

When you are arguing don't speak ill of the other. A word said in anger may be remembered forever. This magnifies the problem and makes it more difficult to return to a good place with one another.

Never criticize another's relationship or marriage. You are not in it. No one knows what goes on between two people.

Does your partner have a good work ethic? Do they show up, do the work, and give one hundred percent? Are they responsible, and do they complete what they begin? This carries over into relationships and home life too.

Is your partner open-minded? Ready to think about new things and accept change? Are they willing to learn new things? Rigid people often see things only one way and are not anxious to do things differently. Remember, rigid thinking can move into the body and causes illness. Take baby steps into new ventures.

It's time to get a written letter of recommendation from his or her father. What does he recommend about his son or daughter? Save it in the book.

Does the person you plan to marry watch porn? Caution! This can be like a drug. This activity can interfere with their ability to relate to a spouse. Porn tends to portray people as sex objects and not human beings. Find a healthy solution.

Do you have a distaste for public displays of affection? That is, hand holding, little kisses, touching. Respect others. Get together on this.

Is he or she prompt? If not, and it drives you crazy, then you either show up later, figure they are worth waiting for, or find someone else. Chances are it is a bad habit, or the person has a less acute sense of time. For the on-time person great patience is required.

Let the past be. There's nothing you can do about it. Live in the NOW. Often silence is golden.

Embrace your differences. They are the spice of your relationship. They will keep you both and interested. They keep you alert and engaged. Enjoy building on a different conversation of your acquaint... of one another.

Are you in love with a twin flame or other multiple times? Prepare to love and live with them within in your life. Better read over this... understand it is our destiny the time bound relationships.

...love the p... ... Strike back. Take time to really know the person you are drawn to. The body language... makes the right... need to find a mental and heart connection for what within... so they will be given free of the truth will... and a person... to find... ... with... with important in your love will... seem.

Embrace your differences. They are the spice of your relationship. They add surprise, fun and interest. They keep you alert and interested. Enjoy making your differences the cornerstone of your acceptance of one another.

Are you in love with a twin, triplet or other multiple birth? Prepare to love and live with their siblings in your life. Better read up on this. Multiple births are usually life time bound relationships.

Love the person, not the body. Take time to really know the person you are drawn to. The body changes. Things can happen. You need to find a mental and heart connection. You want a thrill from their voice, apprecia-tion of their intelligence and a person you crave to be near. Embrace the changes and your love will deepen.

Can you REALLY talk about one another's habits, money, religion, sex, politics, friends, parents, and your heart's desire? You are going to be living with this person a long time. Conversation and communication are as vital as air.

❦

How prepared are you to marry? You need more than love to live. Like money, food, shelter, friends, family, trust, kindness, and faith.

❦

If you are a person who wants to see others happy and content you will be a very good half of a couple. Choose wisely.

Is the man you are marrying like your father?
Is this a good thing? Daughters are very
influenced by their fathers. The familiar is
comfortable even if it wasn't great.

Be aware of this.

Humor diffuses tension and conflict. A
marriage with humor will last longer. Focus
on good news, funny entertainment and
joyful music. Surround yourself with
pleasant people. When this isn't possible,
know that things change and that humor can
lift your spirits. Notice that comedians live
long lives.

Is he a Mama's boy? Is she Daddy's little girl?
If so, be prepared to share your spouse and be
understanding.

If either of you are from a divorced family, think about the relationship that ended. Why did it end? How can your marriage be different? Don't repeat behavior. This is YOUR life and YOUR marriage.

You have to work at marriage every day as you do at your career. Will you get a good review in a year?

Say "I LOVE YOU" to your partner EVERY DAY.

Does your driving scare your partner? Would you want to be afraid every time you got in the car with your spouse? Of course not. So have some respect for your partner's feelings. You will be spending a lot of time in the car.

Will you have a division of labor? If you both work, laundry, housekeeping, and cooking should be shared. How about doing the chores together? Or have a day that you blitz through it all so you have more time to play.

If there is violence in either of your families, get counseling before you marry. Violence is learned by children. Abuse is destructive and has no place in a friendship or a marriage.

To some, sex is just sex. To others, sex is an expression of love. Sex with love is best.

❦

Do you want to share your email, Twitter, Facebook, and chats? Or do you want your privacy? It is important to trust your mate. But if you don't, something must be amiss. If you are suspicious, just ask. Don't snoop.

❦

Which one of you is going to take care of your cars, the house and yard? Both of you should know how to maintain these things. It is important to be self-sufficient. Share the responsibilities and teach one another.

After you marry, combine all your important papers. Learn about taxes, mortgages, insurance, retirement planning and banking. Begin to save money right away.

You are a team, working and loving together.

Does he or she have a roving eye? GROW UP before you marry!

Is there something NOW that he or she does that drives you crazy? If so, it is time to talk about it. Don't be afraid to bring it up or you'll be holding things back all your life.

If someone makes you feel that you are stupid, ugly, incapable, worthless, and doesn't lift you up with their love, this is emotional abuse. You do not need to experience this now or in a marriage. As hard as it may be, move on without this hurtful person.

Handsome is, as handsome does. This goes for beauty too. That is, looks aren't everything. Actions speak louder than looks.

What do your grandparents and aunts and uncles think of this person you plan to marry? Is this important to you?

You must learn to forgive, because you will also need to be forgiven. People are in the process of learning, growing and becoming. There's no perfection. People say the wrong things. They fail and make mistakes. Haven't you? Practice forgiving little things, so if need be, you are stronger for larger issues. Bless your mind and soul by forgiving at the end of every day, and start the next day all new.

Do you hurt your partner with words or actions? Why? It's time to talk about this and change for the better.

Marriage is a man-made institution. The decision to love and care for another is a spiritual bond. Handle lovingly.

When you are married be sure to make sex a priority. Put it on the schedule with work, chores, sports, and getting together with friends and family. Look forward to it. Make time for private time with your partner.

⁂

Say "I appreciate you" every chance you get.

⁂

Ask his or her friends for a written recommendation of the one you will marry. Save it in this book.

You can't change an alcoholic, a drug addict, a gambler, or people with mental health issues. You can help. You can inspire them. But they have to change for themselves.
Sometimes even pure love can't help them. It is an individual experience and requires focus and professional assistance.

⁂

Know your rights. You deserve and are entitled to love and be loved in return. Love yourself and you'll attract love.

⁂

Do you accept who your partner is NOW? Think on this. You know how hard it is to change things about yourself, so what are the chances they will change?

Why are you marrying him or her? Make a
list and write down every reason.

⁂

Negative personalities take a lot of energy to
live with. Either accept this, flow with this, or
leave.

⁂

If you are going to be a step parent you must
talk, talk, talk about what you expect, and
what is expected of you regarding values and
discipline. Be on the same page, and be a
good example for your children. ALWAYS be
kind about the absent parent. Don't make life
harder then it need be for a child.
Children need consistency, safety and two
emotionally stable parents.

Do you dance? Will you be a happier couple if you dance together? Will your partner be very unhappy if you are not dancing with them at celebrations? If your partner won't dance, it's their choice. Get up and enjoy. Most people aren't pros and no one cares how you look dancing.

⁂

If you are prejudiced against certain groups, chances are that you will encounter them within your family. So lighten up and be open to all possibilities. Live your life and let others live theirs.

⁂

Take time for courtship before you marry. Have you seen your partner in all seasons? Talk, date, play.

Who has a great marriage that you personally know? Write down what you like about it and talk about it.

⁂

Have trouble with piercings, tattoos, wigs, toupees, hair transplants, scars, breast implants? Make it known up front.

⁂

Are you interesting? Bored people are usually boring.

Leave work at work. Don't worry about
things you have no control over. Unplug
from all technology at a set time. Be present.
Talk while looking at one another. Take deep
breaths. Be grateful for one another.

What did Mom and Dad tell you about men,
women and marriage? This should be
interesting to talk about.

Beware of Internet romance. Never go alone
to meet a person you have contacted.

Be SMART!

Is he or she a good kisser? Is this important
to you? If so, and your partner is not,
you'd better think about forty, fifty years of
bad kissing.

Until death do us part can be a very long time.
You know when it's right.

Having your own secret signals is romantic.
A wink may mean, "Let's make love tonight."
A hand squeeze at a party may mean "I'm
ready to leave." Your hand on your heart may
say silently, "I love you."

Past loves are past. Release them and
yourself to a new future.

Growing up and growing old together can be
fun. Think positive.

Don't ask questions when you know the
answer might hurt your feelings. "Do I look
good with this mustache?" "Do you like my
tattoo?" "Do these jeans make my butt look
big?"" Think before you speak.

Why does your partner love you? List what is lovable about you.

∼✦∼

Have you done all you have wanted to before you marry? Age one to fifteen is childhood. Age fifteen to twenty-five is figuring things out. Age twenty-five to thirty is prime time.

∼✦∼

No one else can MAKE you happy. They enhance your life and who you are.

When you want something don't nag. If your hints don't work, get your love's attention eye to eye and say, "I want a tennis racket." "I'd like to go out to eat." "It's time to go visit the folks."

❧❧❧

What do you both think about taking in friends or relatives that need temporary help?

❧❧❧

Money is the cause of most divorces. Be smart and plan ahead. What works best for you? Separate checking and savings accounts? Are your debts shared? What is your credit before you are married? Decide how you will pay your bills.

Write your partner love letters on real paper with a pen. Do this often as people express themselves differently, and sometimes better in writing. Everyone enjoys getting love notes. Then they can be read over and over. The Internet is too public and there is no guarantee on privacy.

❦

Anything that bothers you now, that you don't discuss or work out, will possibly still be there five, ten, fifteen years from now. Talk it all out.

❦

Think about a couple that has a horrible relationship. What would you change about it and how? Write it down and talk about it. We learn from others' behavior and mistakes.

Whose last name will you use when you marry? His or hers? Both of yours hyphenated? Or will you make up a new name? (It's been done.) Do consider your families' feelings.

How will you deal with arguments? Talk them out? Pout? Discuss with everyone but your spouse? If it is serious, get help. Everyone needs guidance now and then.

Don't discuss past romances. It's disheartening and serves no positive purpose. This relationship now is your top priority.

will you have an open door policy with your

Will you have an open door policy with your in-laws? Discuss this with both your partner and in-laws. Everyone does better when everyone knows the boundaries. Your in-laws will have their expectations too.

What is your partner's worst habit? Can you live with it?

How do you feel about adopting children?

Women, if you plan to have children, do not marry a man who you would have to "ask" to babysit HIS children. An involved father will be able to take over in a minute and know all he needs to about his child for their comfort and safety.

❧❦❧

Sex evolves. Are you flexible and willing to try new things? Variety is the spice of life.

❧❦❧

Don't compare what you have or who you are with others. Be yourself.

Discuss in detail how you will save and spend
money. Write it down and make a plan.

Practicing your faith together and celebrating
your religious events is a great way to keep a
marriage strong. Prayer is positive thinking
and being grateful. Try it, it works.

Some people treat their friends better than
their partners. Is this you? Then STOP
because your husband or wife should be your
best friend. Remember you have to be a
friend to have one.

Do you like to have parties and have family and friends over to visit? It is great fun and both are important to your relationship. It's even better if you BOTH enjoy it.

It can't hurt, and might help, to look at your astrology signs. It is another tool to understand better those we love.

Is your partner critical of you and others? Sometimes this is just a bad habit. Otherwise, it's immature and unkind and can be very destructive to your marriage.

You are what you think. How is your self-image? What is your image as a couple?

What do you want it to be?

How do you handle stress? By screaming, drinking, drugs, anger, abuse? Run from these. Learning anger management, yoga, meditation, exercising, and sports will help you deal with stress.

Do you agree on how to play? Share one another's choice of entertainment, hobbies, and sports and support one another. Think about how you want to spend your free time. Having things in common is a plus.

How do you feel about inviting the widow next door, the single guy at work, or your aging aunt for the holiday celebrations? It could be you someday.

Can you talk about sex and what you like and don't like? What you desire, think, and feel intimately? Talking about it is important.

You each need a private space. Everyone needs a thinking spot. Consider a den, a home office, your own bathroom, the garage.

Some people won't go to funerals, hospitals or nursing homes. Would this upset you if your partner had this aversion?

❧❧❧

People see money differently. It is very important to agree on how you save and spend money.

❧❧❧

Does your partner learn from mistakes, or the hard way, having to make many mistakes before they "get it"? Look around and observe how others handle problems. It could save you some time and pain.

Being with family and friends gives you the opportunity to brag about your partner's achievements. "Mary got a promotion!" "Joe ran a marathon!" "My wife is a great cook." Appreciation goes a long way and it strengthens your relationship.

⚬⚬⚬

Touch your partner often. Touch reaches the heart. It's healthy too.

⚬⚬⚬

What's your partner's family background temperament? Different cultures react differently to problems. Some are highly emotional and other very quietly stoic. Understanding what makes them tick is important to how you will react.

Are you the kind of person you would want to be with?

Beware of drugs. They weaken the mind and body and can destroy those surrounding you.

What type of parent will your partner be? They will be a role model for your children. Not everyone is cut out to be a parent. Will he be a great father? Will she be a great mother?

What kind of life do you want? Anything is

❧

❧

they apologize and be sorry? If not, there is a
huge problem.

What kind of life do you want? Anything is possible. Can you make it happen together?

Don't be afraid to be picky about who you marry! It is YOUR life.

Does your partner have a conscience? Can they apologize and be sorry? If not, there is a huge problem.

Everyone does better when they feel good, look good, are approved of and complimented. Help your partner by saying how much you love and appreciate them.

Think twice before you marry someone who is a big spender or extremely frugal unless you are too. Different spending styles can make you miserable.

When you have children and they see that you care for others, you're a good example. They may take care of you someday.

How does your partner measure up to what
you had in mind for a spouse?

Treat your partner as you would your most
precious friend.

Melding families takes time. Are you
comfortable with their family? Your
partner's peace of mind is at stake.

Remember, your partner's family raised the person you love. Not everyone gets along. Effort is admirable.

What's most important to you? A clean house or a home cooked meal? Often time doesn't allow for both. Relax.

Learn to talk and listen to one another. In years to come, you'll want someone more to talk to than have sex with.

Everything you expect in him or her, do you expect of yourself?

❧

Is he a gentleman? He should not belch, fart, spit, pick his nose, or adjust himself in front of you or in public! Guys, just leave the room to take care of this business and always wash your hands before leaving the men's room.

❧

Is she a lady? Does she sit with her legs crossed, chew with her mouth closed, and speak kindly? Does she use foul language? Is she well-groomed, polite and thoughtful?

For same sex couples who can't get married, and couples who don't want to marry see the practical tips in the book *The Essential Guide to Living Together as an Unmarried Couple* by Dorlan.

Wifely experience advice. Don't buy a man a reclining chair.

Husbandly advice. Don't ever buy an appliance for a birthday, anniversary, Valentine's Day or Christmas/Hanukah. Make it personal.

Do not be subservient to your husband or wife for your children's sake. Have respect for your spouse. Consult and compromise. Your children will learn from your example how good relationships work.

Does he or she have children already? This is huge. The children will be members of your family and their other parent will always be in your life. There are many books that deal with parenting stepchildren. Be prepared. Expect your spouse to support their children with time and money. How could you love someone who didn't?

If the person you plan to marry recently ended a relationship, broke off an engagement, or is widowed, it is important for them to have time to heal and grieve. Give them time to think about their past relationship, and be secure in their new direction. You don't want to be the rebound guy or gal.

Thinking of becoming engaged and married?
Start saving ten percent of your income now.
Don't stop. Pay yourself first! Continue this
through your life.

Is it important to you to celebrate birthdays,
Valentine's Day, Sweetest Day? If it isn't,
make it known to the one you love so you are
not disappointed. Some people and families
do not make a big deal of these days. Look at
them as one more chance to express your love.
Or, agree that you are not going to buy cards
and gifts or do anything special.

Once you are known as a couple, both of you keep a calendar. Mark your special days. Check it every day. It's nice to be thoughtful of parent's birthdays, the anniversary of when you met, important dates and appointments. It shows you care.

Can you and your partner talk about death? Yours, and others? Tomorrow is not for sure. What are your wishes about organ donation, burial, cremation? Give your partner the information they need. It will make their lives easier in a difficult time.

Every married couple expects their marriage to last until old age. Things happen. Life changes. Divorce is not the end of the world. BUT, if you are being damaged, or are damaging others and children, be brave and smart and separate. Talking about this now may help in difficult times. Love is making another's life better not worse. Write your thoughts on this.

If one of you is a perfectionist, and the other is not, does trouble lie ahead? What you think is "cute" now, could be grounds for divorce in about two years. One of you lighten up, or accept it.

Thou shalt not commit adultery. This doesn't mean that you can't find other people attractive. Your choice to be married however, means that you don't want to ruin the relationship you are creating, and therefore will reject things that can destroy it.

Do you see marriage as a fairy tale? The wedding is the beginning of the work of your marriage. You must put the same energy and passion into it as you would a sport or a career. "Happily Ever After" is not possible since no one is perfect.

Do you have tact? That is, knowing when to say and not to say things. Think before you speak. Think how others will feel after you speak.

Attraction to the strong silent type is short lived. You'll be in counseling soon yelling "He/she never talks to me!"

Is your love conscious about their physical, mental, emotional and spiritual health? When you are young, it's easy to say "yes". Have a physical exam before you marry. Check resentments and anger and find ways to deal with hurt and stress.
Emotions are reactions to what happens. How do you react? Do you have a spiritual belief? Think on this. It is the foundation of who you are.

Do you believe in family planning? Abortion?
Are you ready to put yourself aside and care
for another person? Get all the information
you need. Know how your bodies work.
Discuss family size and the kind of family
you want to have.

Surprises happen, but you can be in control.
Both men and women need to be
knowledgeable about birth control. There's
no reason not to be with all the information
on the Internet. Don't be shy. This is family
planning. Ask questions.

Don't be afraid to ask questions. Millions of
people have lived before you and answers are
available. You don't know everything. No one
does. Get on a computer. Search for books.
Ask experts in your area for life advice.

Have you had sex before with another person? If you are in any doubt and really love your partner have a blood test for STD's It is simple, quick and cheap, and will save an ocean of heartache.

❧

If you are from different races, there may be more obstacles to your life's harmony.

Talk to both of your families. Discuss in depth your differences and expectations.

❧

Some people are very politically minded. Will you cancel one another out at the polls? Do you care? Register to vote!

Are you marrying for love, money, security, companionship or because everybody else is doing it? Seriously, make a list. Talk about this. If you can't talk about it you have a stumbling block.

Are you forgiving? Be gentle with one another. Try not to create a situation where you have to forgive or be forgiven.

Women, learn to care for the car, mow the yard, how the furnace and A/C work, and home maintenance tips. You should understand the mortgage, insurance, retirement and credit, and you should have a will prepared to protect the ones you love. Men of course should know how the washer and dryer work, how to do laundry, cook, run the vacuum, care for the children, and keep up with family and friends. If one day you have to take care of it all, you will do so easily.

Stay out of other people's marriages. What if they interfered with yours?

***

There's a lot to the saying, "The best way to a man's heart is through his stomach."
At the end of the day, everyone is tired and hungry. They just want to be listened to and fed. It's an excellent habit to come together for a meal at the end of the day. Both of you put your energies together and make it happen. What works for your work schedule and life style?

***

With whom do you feel safest? Why? Talk about it.

Do you respect one another's opinions? This is vital. You share space and energy. You don't have to have the same opinions, just respect them.

If you are a person that repeats jokes and stories over and over again in front of your love, stop it! Would you want to listen to you?

Keep old friends but always be open for new ones. A strong marriage thrives in friendship support. Couples don't always like the same people. Try patience and tolerance.

Find out all about your partner's childhood.
These were the years that influenced them
and made them who they are. Share your
remembrances, the good and not so good.

⊰❧⊱

Sex is good between two consenting adults.
It's your intimate communication. Variety is
the spice of life.

⊰❧⊱

Wouldn't it be lovely to die in one another's
arms smiling? Live in one another's arms
smiling.

Absence makes the heart grow fonder, if you're not gone too long! Sharing experiences and life committed to one another keeps a marriage vital and growing. Long absences place a burden on you both even though today's technology is so wonderful. Touching is important.

***

Say please and thank you! You'd be surprised how far these words will take you.

***

Right now, realize that thousands of studies have been done about men and women being different. Be glad of this. It's a balance. Enjoy the person you love.

Does your partner lie? This is serious. It means they are insecure and that they need to be important. Liars lead complicated lives. They have to make up stuff constantly. This may be a creative mind, but one who is misusing it and your trust.

$$\infty\mathcal{G}\mathcal{G}\infty$$

Loss of a job and financial worries put great stress on a relationship. Your security is threatened. Be patient and be hopeful. Get as much education as you can. Be positive and supportive. Make the most of your talents.

$$\infty\mathcal{G}\mathcal{G}\infty$$

Be prepared. Are you able to take care of yourself before you get married? That is, food, shelter and clothing.
Being self-sufficient should not be a threat to your love.

You don't know what life has in store.

Do you think of little ways to treat or surprise your partner? This is a fun habit to get into. Small favors and kindnesses spark the heart of the giver and the receiver. It adds joy to your relationship.

❦

Take time to do nothing; either together or alone. It's a busy world. Everyone needs slow time, rest and comfort.

❦

You want to be anxious to be with the one you love. You want to think of them when you are at work or away. Nurturing your relationship is important. Look one another in the eyes often.

Everyone does not plan to, or want to be
married. Respect their choice and include
them in your life. The more the merrier.

Plan your wedding together! It's a day you
BOTH make a commitment to one another.
Make lists and have fun doing it. Don't let the
details cause you both stress. The
anticipation is longer than the event, and
the memories are forever.

Remember we can't always be loved the
way we wish. Count your blessings. Often
in relationships one is the lover and one is
the lovee.

All relationships are not meant to last forever. Know your partnerships with the present energy and do your best.

All relationships are not meant to last forever. Enter your marriage with the best energy and do your best.

We all like to be noticed and praised. It costs you nothing to compliment the person closest to you. Find a way to do this every day. This thoughtfulness will come back to you.

Be constructive. Don't criticize. You know how much you love to be criticized.

Be neat and clean and huggable. Wash your
hands, brush your teeth, and smell good.
Greet your love with a smile.

⁂

If you are having the same arguments over
and over again, it's time to decide if it's worth
the energy. Do you just want to be right or in
control? Everyone is entitled to their
opinion. Declaring a truce and letting go is
a good move in many areas in your life. Why
keep alive a dead end argument?

⁂

Don't give up easily. Try, try again.

Ask a sibling for a recommendation of your
partner. Save it in this book.

Siblings will tell you the truth.

❧⦿❧

Don't assume ANYTHING! Open your mouth
and ask. Save yourself a lot of grief.

❧⦿❧

How were you disciplined as a child? All
children are different and should be
disciplined according to their individuality. Be
fair. Talk to your intended about your ideas
of raising children. Read up on child rearing
before children come.

Be prepared.

Never say, "My child will never do that." They
will for sure.

Two minds and hearts are better than one.
Combine your talents for fun and prosperity.

Take care of yourself so you can express your

Never say "My child will never do that!" They will for sure.

Two minds and hearts are better than one. Combine your talents for fun and prosperity.

Take care of yourself so you can express your love a long, long time.

Do you want a partner that is a clinging vine?
If so, you will make them an emotional
cripple. Encourage their independence.
Clinging gets old and will erode a marriage.

Be careful what you wish for.
You may get it tenfold.

If your partner is a recent widow or widower,
give them time to grieve. That is, unless you
are up in years. In this case, don't wait too
long, time is short.

Do you dislike the mountains or the beach?
Car travel or camping? You'd better discuss
this now. Maybe separate vacations will work.

What if one of your children is gay? Marries
another race? Adopts children from another
country? These things happen every day.
Love SHOULD be unconditional. Meaning "I
love you no matter what." Before you marry
talk about these situations and how you think
and feel about them.

Think of long married couples you know.
What do you like about how they act and
treat one another? How they are just didn't
happen. Deep relationships take time.

Men should have a basic understanding of women's menses, changes that happen in pregnancy, and menopause. These hormonal fluctuations do effect often how women feel and react. Talk about it. The more information you have, the more helpful you can be. Women are different through these natural hormonal changes.

※

Most problems between couples boil down to changing, accepting or detaching. Try to be open minded in all discussions. Don't say "No" right away. Think about it.

Detaching means ignoring or leaving.

※

For an interesting life and marriage it is best that you both have friends, hobbies and social groups. All these will enhance your lives together.

The secret of good real estate is location, location, location. The secret of a good marriage is compromise, compromise, compromise.

Women should read up on men's anatomy and how it works. You'll be glad you did.

Try and eat a meal together every day. Talk and eat, talk and eat. But not with your mouth full!

Is he or she controlling? Why? And, why would you allow someone to control you? Look at their background. Will you be comfortable for years and years under someone's thumb?   Think seriously about this and choose wisely.

⁂

Do you have credit cards? Do you use them wisely? Sometimes divorces are harder to get than credit. Don't "borrow" trouble.

⁂

When men reach forty-ish they may question their life and work and what it's been all about. Often they just want change. Start talking about this at about age thirty-five and don't stop. Work at keeping your life interesting for both of you.

...re you made or given about your...
...cloth... hair? Are you together on what you
both want and how to get it?

...Does your partner defend you? Have they
spoken up for you when people criticize you,
...condescending, and criticize "all that"?

...and... a low energy person...
...Couples who are... similar will be...
...two very energetic people... and...
...and... constant...

Are you image driven about your house, car, clothes, boat? Are you together on what you both want and how to get it?

Does your partner defend you? Have they spoken up for you when people are rude, judgmental, and critical? Will they?

Are your energies closely matched? A very energetic person and a low energy person often don't understand the other's needs. Couples whose energies are similar will be most comfortable together. But, be aware that two very energetic, active people may burn one another out and be on a constant search for change.

Can your partner apologize? These are sweet
words that let you know you are thought
about and cared for.

Would your love rather be right or happy?
"Right" is short lived if you are not happy.

Love is everything. It makes us and breaks
us. It is vital to our well-being, physical and
mental health. We all want it and need it.
Once you are blessed to have it with a partner,
it MUST be maintained. You can't be lazy
and let it ride. It involves learning to know,
respect and explore the other person who
is, like you, a constant work in progress and
ever changing.

Do you enjoy shopping together? To some it is an event and to others, torture.

Do what you love best. Help out now and then or share the chore of grocery and gift shopping.

❦

Are there family secrets? Should they remain so or be discussed? Does it matter that Aunt Louise is transgender? That cousin Bob is adopted? That there was a suicide? Health problems and criminal activities should be out in the open. This information is important for the welfare of the family.

❦

Does your partner love their work? Many people are defined by their work. Are you both supportive of your career choices?

Food for thought. Does he have a sister? Does she have a brother? These sibling experiences helps in understanding of men and women.

Are you cousins? Contrary to popular belief, cousins, even first cousins, can marry. Laws vary from state to state. In some cultures it is a favored marriage. Go to genetic counseling if you want to have children. Check on the Internet for this type of counseling nearest you.

Do you think you are Gay? Be fair and be honest. Explore this before you marry.

Don't ruin years of your life and another's. You both deserve to be with someone who loves you for exactly who you are.

The average workplace is not compatible with modern family life. When two parents work, who is doing all the things that need to be done to care for a child properly? Family, day care, babysitter? Some employers have flexible hours. Explore your options.

❧❦❧

There are stay-at-home moms, and stay-at-home dads. The first three years of a loving parent raising their child is invaluable to their start in life.

❧❦❧

Are you ready to welcome a child? Are you a good communicator with your spouse?

If you have practiced solving conflicts you
have a good foundation for parenting.

It is loving teamwork.

Be aware that some people have to warm up
to the idea of parenting. Talk, talk, talk about
it together. How do you REALLY feel about
it? This is not a crime for either. Know what
you both want and discuss it at length.

What do you think life will be like when you
have a baby? Talk to couples you know who
have a child and ask how their lives changed.
It WILL change. This is good change. Life is
change. Be secure in your love for one
another as there will be less time for the two
of you. You will want to schedule dates to
talk and rejoice.

Men, know NOW, that sexual intimacy WILL
change after the baby comes.

Help the new mother get sleep and nurture
her. She will be ready for sex if you do.

After the baby arrives, there may be loss of
income from mom's job, loss of freedom, loss
of intimacy. Babies are TOTALLY dependent
on mom and dad. You will have to WORK at
romance.

You won't be the first two people to have a
baby. Use your instincts. Protect and love
your partner. Does your partner do this now?

Families do things together. Talk about your vision of what things you want to do with your family. Experiences you want to have and share. What things did you enjoy doing with your family growing up?

⁂

Families support each other's dreams. A strong parent bond begins this. Your family comes first. What do you think about this?

⁂

This is being repeated because it is SO important: Be able to say "I am sorry", "I forgive you", "I love you". These words are vital for those you love the most to hear. Be generous in your heart and soul with these words.

Lovers, partners, and friends say "We." How lovely to share your life with someone you love. You are free individuals, but stand together as "We."

Strong relationships are flexible on every day matters. Do you sweat the small stuff? Or, do you go with the flow?

Women, train your husband from day one! Especially if your mother-in-law didn't do the job. There's the laundry, tooth paste cap, wet wash cloth, toilet seat, socks on the floor, toilet paper roll, gas in the car, greeting cards and thank you notes, table clearing and parenting. It seems like common sense that these tasks would be shared. But not if someone else has taken care of them all their life. Early learning tip: Give a choice. "Honey, would you rather fold the laundry or do the dishes?" Be sure then to be the best future mother-in-law by teaching your son to be a good and thoughtful husband one day.

Happy people are accepting, flexible, constructively busy, can forgive and share. Do you surround yourself with happy people?

Happy people have friends and family. If you don't have these, do you want to create it?

Good feelings are thoughts acted upon. Share your thoughts. Anticipate your partner's needs. Have you done this lately?

Everyone feels better when they can do what they love best. Think of what thrills you and pleases you. What work or activity makes you happiest?

Have either of you had to persevere through difficult times? Share this with one another so they know you better. Getting through adversity once, helps the next time you are challenged.

What are you grateful for? Being grateful enlarges happiness.

Can you forgive hurts? Sometimes, it's
extremely hard to do. Can you let go and
know that you too may need someone to
forgive you sometime?

Do you draw negative things to you with
negative thoughts? You can also draw good
things to you with positive thoughts.

Try it NOW.

You only have the NOW. So, be careful in
what you say and do and how you act.

Let love expand your life. Act nice and you'll
get nice back. Try it, you'll like it.

⁂

Avoid the words ALWAYS and NEVER. These
are huge words. They usually are critical
and make another feel bad about themselves.
Pinpoint what you want without a negative
use of these words. An example: You
ALWAYS scream at me.

Pinpoint: I would like it if you spoke quietly
about what you want.

⁂

Are you able to make sacrifices for the one you
love? Perhaps she does not enjoy car races, or
he attending plays. Do you go to please your
partner? Maybe you rise early to have more
time with one another before a busy day?
These are priceless gifts of yourself. Think of
little ways to please the one you love.

No job lasts forever, but your family does.
Make time with them a priority.

※

Again, don't assume anything! Open your
mouth and ask. "Am I supposed to take a dish
to your mother's on Sunday?" "Are you
playing golf on Saturday?" "What did the
doctor tell you?" "Is there gas in the car?"
Don't make another guess or try to read your
mind. Speak up.
This will make your life easier.

※

Can you see beyond your own pain and see the
needs of others? You are a part of the family
of mankind. Others may have done this
for you.

Show appreciation for a smile, a kiss, clean laundry, a made bed, time for your favorite TV show. This way you will get more of all you want.

⁂

If you must criticize, do so kindly. There are always two ways to say things.

"That outfit is interesting." "Your mother had a different take on the kids today."

"I'll use your toothbrush since you're using mine."

⁂

Does your relationship raise many questions and meet with disapproval from your family and friends? If so, your future could be rocky. It's best to take time to talk to family and friends and find out why. Passion is short-lived. What do they see that you don't?

Do you want to live together without being married? Read *Unmarried To Each Other: The Essential Guide to Living Together as an Unmarried Couple* by Dorian Solot and Marshall Miller.

If you are very young and getting married remember that you can grow together or apart. At twenty-seven, you are not the same as you were at seventeen. Experiences help you grow. What kind of marriage do you want in ten years?

Often young people marry because their home life is unhappy and they want to get away from it and be loved. Discuss how your family life will be better or different from the one you left. How will you make this happen?

It's easy to love a healthy, fun, working person. If they are ill and out of work, what bonds will help you stand by until your life is "fun" again? Talk about this.

✦

Are you a better person in or out of this relationship?

✦

To be compatible with another you must be willing to work at sharing the spirit of your soul, keep a good disposition, and over and over again, day after day, be present, alert and flexible. Compatibility doesn't just happen.

Do you feel obligated to marry this person? Maybe now is just not the right time.

✧✦✧

Yes, it's true that when you are in love you just KNOW it. When it's right, deep down, you feel comfortable. It "sits" right with you. If in doubt, don't.

✧✦✧

How do you feel when you are with your partner? List your feelings and share them with one another.

Do you have hidden doubts? Is there a
nagging in your mind? If so, then
something needs to change.

❧

Be alert if there is abuse in either of
your families. Unfortunately this behavior
is often learned and may enter into your
relationship. It is best to get professional
help if you are intent on marrying. Physical
violence is NEVER to be tolerated.
If you have not had this problem before
marrying, and then do after, even if it is a
week later, LEAVE and get help.

❧

Plan ahead. Where do you see yourselves in
five years? Ten years? Goals are good. Are
you thinking toward the same goals?

It is important to share values about family, money, education, spirituality and your outlook on fellow human beings. These are core issues that make up who you are.

How do you feel about moving to another state or country? Can you expect this from your job at some point in time? Not everyone wants to be away from friends and family. However beginning somewhere new can strengthen your relationship. Communication is so easy today. Be flexible.

If your partner doesn't like to travel, go to movies, eat out, shop, explore outdoor adventures, what will you do together or apart? Contrary to the popular saying "Opposites attract", this is not true. Couples with common interests will enrich their relationship by spending more time together and sharing activities.

Do not measure one another by other people! Every individual is unique. Accept the other person for who they are or move on. Comparisons destroy self-esteem, and are unfair, and very destructive. You do not truly love this person if you have to compare them.

Don't let others sabotage your relationship. Make it clear that you do not appreciate their interference. Friends and family should want the best for you both.

Be brave enough to love. "Nothing ventured, nothing gained." And you could pass up something wonderful. Be worthy of another's love.

If negative feelings get in the way, get them out! Say them out loud. Then they become less powerful and doable. Try it.

❧

Don't jump to conclusions! Get more information. Keep your imagination in check and go to the source. Example: Bill tells Bob that he saw Mary at lunch with Tim. Just ask Mary who Tim is.

❧

Celebrate often. Sometimes love flows, sometimes it struggles. Either way, recognize it out loud with a flourish. It feels good.

According to Dr. Kevin Leman, author of *Birth Order Connection,* the best matches are an only child and a youngest, the oldest child and the youngest, and the middle child and the youngest. The absolute best being an only female child or first born marrying the youngest male with older sisters. The not so great combinations are middle child to middle child, last child to last child, only female to only male and a first born female with no brothers and a last born male with no sisters. For in depth explanations check out Dr. Leman's book.

Visualize and plan abundance in all things. Expecting blessings is easier on the mind and heart than expecting nothing.

You agree to come together. Then, agree to separate if that day comes. Be fair. Be kind. Some relationships run their course and it's time to move on.

How will you pay for the rent, phone, electricity, water, insurance, food gas, clothes and entertainment? Work hard, love hard, play hard and laugh a lot.

She is a vegetarian, he's a beefeater! Does love conquer all? It depends on who is doing the cooking. You have to eat. Talk it over.

She prefers dogs. He prefers cats. What will you do? Is it possible you can adapt to your partner's favorite? Pets are wonderful to have. You don't know unless you try.

Remember you're not the creator of things, those smells, feelings, debts, or intimacy. It's _____ that's hard to deal if that time heart of love will ____

Do make time to be totally alone with your partner at least once a week, just to say, "How are you?"

Be observant and listen. When it you make plans for a special date, choose what the person of your desire would like to do, the activity not what you'd pick it and that they may not want _____ computing.

Be aware if he or she is afraid of bugs, dogs, snakes, water, heights, debt, or intimacy. It's time to deal with it, or learn to live with it.

Do make time to be totally alone with your partner at least once a week, just to say "How are you?"

Be observant and listen. When you make plans for a special date, choose what the person of your desire would like to do. She may not want to go bowling and he may not want to go antiquing.

Be yourself, but learn to compromise. You
only look good when you do. When both give,
both get.

What is his view of women's rights? What
is her view of men? Respect is vital. When
respect is lost, love soon is lost.

Give up greed and selfishness. It is the cause
of personal misery.

Are you compassionate? Can you empathize with others, put yourself in their place, and realize everyone needs the same things that you do? Compassion puts the passion in a relationship.

Another tool to understanding your love is *Linda Goodman's Love Signs*. It is about your astrological sign. Try it. You might like it. You may discover why your partner is ambitious or a home body. Use all the information at your fingertips.

No one can make you feel a certain way unless you LET them. If your partner says "You make me angry!" Ask them to take responsibility for their feelings. It should be, "I am angry!" Then find out why and what can dissolve the anger.

Is your partner capable of turning a negative into a positive? This is a person who can bounce back and look at the bright side of things.

Be clear about what you believe and what you stand for. Think about who you are and express it honestly.

Know that problems are experiences that give you reason to learn and grow. They teach us life lessons and to do better.

Grow in the same direction together.

Support the one you love in their hopes,
dreams, goals and difficulties. They will do
the same for you.

Build memories together and then lose your
memories together in old age.

Your wedding day is another day in your life of growing. All the days that follow will not be romantic. Do not set up unrealistic expectations of marriage. Emotional maturity says, "Life changes and I accept new experiences."

MOST women would rather be talked to than made love to! And after making love, men do NOT want to be talked to.

MOST men are boys inside full of mischief and play. Women, tend to the man and the boy.

be responsible for your own happiness and

Don't tell your partner how miserable they

Don't expect the one you love to "save you."
Be responsible for your own happiness and
enhance other's.

Don't tell your partner how miserable they
make you. Tell them what you want.

This works better.

Marriage was a man-made idea for joining
names and property. This old idea is long
past. Hopefully your marriage will be a
joining of great friends learning and
growing together.

If your premarital relationship is physical try
abstaining for a few weeks and see how things
go. It is difficult, but you will learn a lot about
each other.

Learn to let your beloved be the focus of your
attention for a few minutes each day.
Actively listen to what they have to say.
Practice hearing "beyond their words"
and try to understand their perspective.

Nothing in this world remains static. Our
world is constantly changing and so are we.
Look at these inevitable changes as an
opportunity to discover something new
about each other. Explore how the person
in your life has changed during the
time that you have known each other.

Never be shy or afraid to ask questions.
Millions of people have lived before you and
your answers are available. You don't know
everything. No one does. Get on a computer.
Search for books. Ask experts in your area for
life advice.

❦

Are you ready to trust and share? Marriage is
a partnership. Two become one. One's pain is
the other's. One's joy is the other's.

❦

Every anniversary, take this book out
and review it. Discuss what has happened
over the past year and what you liked and
didn't like. Then talk about what you can do
differently and what you both want. Maybe
make some notes. Every year, different things
will be important to you.

❦

Be good to one another every day and you will
bask in a greater friendship, respect and love.
And, whatever you do, do it lovingly.

LOVE

Love is patient. Love is kind.
Love is not jealous, it does not
put on airs, it is not
snobbish. Love is never rude,
it is not self-seeking, it is not
prone to anger; neither does it
brood over injures. Love does
not rejoice in what is wrong,
but rejoices with the truth.
There is no limit to love's
forbearance, its truth, its hope,
its power to endure...There are
in the end three things that
last: faith, hope, and love, and
the greatest of these is love.

St. Paul to the Corinthians

Indian Wedding Prayer

Now you will feel no rain,
for each of you will be
shelter for the other.

Now there is no more
loneliness.

Now you are two persons,
but there is only one life
before you.

May your days together
be good and long upon the
earth.

www.ingramcontent.com/pod-product-compliance
Lightning Source LLC
Chambersburg PA
CBHW060031030426
42334CB00019B/2282